CALL *and* RESPONSE

CALL *and* RESPONSE

Rob Carney

www.blacklawrence.com

Executive Editor: Diane Goettel
Book Design: Amy Freels
Cover Design: Zoe Norvell
Cover Art: "Clear Mind Overture" by Duy Huynh

Published 2021 by Black Lawrence Press.
Printed in the United States.

CONTENTS

I.

POETIC JUSTICE

This happened on November 9th
in Salt Lake City

on the corner of 500 North
and Morton Drive,

a spot that used to be in Mexico,
and before that

a tribal footpath, crossing from the mountains
to a million migratory birds.

•

Rewind from there and you'll see mastodons,
mastodons sensing

that the air has changed:
no spring on the way

with its snowmelt grasses,
or violets coming

like the Earth's best secret, violets
they've been waiting all winter to eat.

•

Walk it back more
and it's the home of crabs, sideways stepping

through tide pools,
the corner of 5th North and Morton

on the Inland Sea.
It helps to remember.

●

Anyway, after the ballots were counted,
a Somali girl, walking to school, fifth grade,

her head and hair covered as always,
was happy about her teacher,

or noticing the weather,
or thinking that burnt toast smelled too familiar...

like that Red Cross ambulance
hit by a mortar...

when the crossing guard, holding his sign out, said,
"Enjoy your free flight back to the jungle."

•

I don't know what her backpack weighed,
but carrying that moment around all day—

and in her memory
forever—

probably felt like shouldering
a broken moon,

.

though that's not the end of the story

•

because a dire wolf
(long extinct, but not today)

turned that white man
into bloody screaming.

Throat gone first. Then his liver.
Then part of a thigh.

•

He resurrected.
He had no memory of being eaten.

He stood in the crosswalk, feeling accomplished,
like a star.

Then the ghost of Shakespeare appeared.
He was looking for a half-wit to cast as Polonius.

"Step behind this curtain," he said.
"I need to see

if you're stab-able."
Turned out he was.

•

The crossing guard
came back from the dead,

this time facing a firing squad.
He'd insulted the daughter of a hacienda owner,

and a nun planting corn at the orphanage,
and women from Syria, Somalia,

from Bosnia, Cambodia,
from Poland and Ireland and fleeing

the Confederate South.
He'd insulted the trees who'd heard him.

And the future
for being in its history.

And even the ore taken out of a mountain,
then heated and shaped

into the shovel head
waiting nearby.

•

When he stood up, lit by the morning,
the bison stampeding him were beautiful,

as if the mountains had decided to run downhill
and out across the valley.

His dying thought while lying there—
a bird's nest

of compound fractures—
was *Where the hell did those buffalo come from?*

But that was wrong; buffalo are in Asia.
His face was in the dirt.

•

He sat up quickly and got to his feet.
His clothes weren't even dusty.

It was post-election Wednesday,
near Meadowlark Elementary,

and all the kids from the neighborhood
were headed his way.

He didn't much care for the black girl's *hijab*,
said, "Enjoy your free flight back to the jungle,"

but instead of sidewalks or African forests
there was water, an inland sea.

At the surface above him were silhouettes:
kids' windmill arms, and legs kicking.

It would've been nice to do that too,
but he couldn't swim.

•

He resurrects again,
unaware of drowning,

and a flock of ocean liners flies across the sky,
sounding impossible,

like Salvador Dalí painting with thunder,
a painting titled *Migratory Birds*.

Somehow the huge ships misjudge the distance,
drop anchor

and veer on their wings
two miles before the lake, skid down

atop the crossing guard: barnacled hulls,
and concrete, and him in between.

•

Something quiet flutters now
in the shadow

cast by one of them.
It's a red-and-white fabric sign on a stick.

It says, "STOP."

II.
9 JOURNEYS

"ART IS SUCH A GOOD JOURNEY"

Kari's grandmother used to tell us,
"Put some scribbles there—

a million begonias.
And now it's spring again, blooming. Yes."

Not scuba,
not yoga,

not for her,
but she could make you young-eyed

when teaching you to paint.
"Orange pinwheels, try it,

that's sunlight,
that's Mama Eggs." And my favorite,

what I'll never forget:
"Don't ever put your vision on

like shoes, my darlings. We're traveling,
not making doormats."

"WHAT ARE YOUR SKILLS?"

Every year at Sea School
we were taught that glaciers purr

and ice floes, huge
below the surface, were sunning cats.

Call ours a failed education.
If it makes you feel better,

call our hymns under night skies
cracked.

But for thirteen years
we sailed on bluer water.

And all of us know well
how to arch our backs.

"ARE YOU HUNGRY?"

Paul's grandfather fell
from his house in the air

when his dreaming turned to birds.
Sometimes it means you'll find a hawk's egg,

and others it just means listen to the river
saying, "Start in my stream

below the mountain's scar,
and ignore the bears around you.

Float still, a leaf, then find
momentum. You'll gain the whole sea."

Midnight visions
are a common kind of travel,

whether *just a journey*
or *a finding.*

But you can't peg orders, can't call the shots,
or dreams stall, lose power,

maybe drop you
from your tree house. You'll land

in an empty kitchen,
wanting bread.

"TELL US ONE OF YOUR RECIPES"

If they say, "Turn left
at the wind's nest,"

that's a tree. Its bark
is just bark, so don't get lost,

don't listen
to their nine names for whatnot.

If they tell you their rain
is the most skilled kind,

then walk away.
Already, your food should taste better.

"HOW DO YOU PLAY?
WHAT'S THE SCORE?"

Begin by pinning seven talismans
to Night's backyard.

By rule, this is called
the Big Dipper.

By rule, you must notice that the air
stays almost warm.

Come morning, the birds will spiral.
Under vines, the ground

will thaw.
Rocks persist,

and skeletons,
but not snow.

All of us know this. That's the rule.
Interest is temporary.

Points are deducted.
There's always a waning moon.

"STILL WORKS GOOD. BEST OFFER"

Someone's selling a futon.
Just the frame.

It's broken, it's raining,
it's on the lawn.

I don't have much worth much—
86 cents, and a CD

that skips on track 9—
but we strike a bargain.

Sometimes you knock and doors open.
Sometimes they're home.

Now I sit as the cars pass by, red and blue
and purposeful.

Possibly their drivers wonder
why I'm holding a dripping sign.

"I'VE STILL GOT MY PASSPORT"

Don't take this personally—
I'm sure you think you understand fire,

and it's true some forests stir up
out of ash; everything leafy—

but I liked me better
as a wooded slope,

and you far more
in your riverbed,

when we were an unnamed country.
And no one had a map.

"WHEN'S MY LUCK GONNA CHANGE?"

There aren't enough miracles
to divvy up.

Sometimes
this frustrates the angels.

They'd like to build a motor
that rewinds chances, swing

a wrecking ball at the vertebrae
of bad luck,

but they aren't industrial;
they just sing.

I'm not complaining. They're nice hosts,
but what can they do?

Storms blast. The sky goes on.
They wish us well.

"HAPPY NEW YEAR!"

The New Year laughs in the street.
He's not wearing a hat.

He yells, "Nothing to see here,
I'm just snowing"...

someone better go and ask him in.
Go *pronto* or he'll keep this up,

snowing from block
to block,

and aren't there enough drunks already?
Like we need one more?

Hurry up now, hug him, bring him
inside; we all know he means well.

We'll get the New Year some coffee.
He can purr by the fire.

III.

IN THE BEGINNING WAS A RIVER

People who know me know this: I don't pretend to be an expert on the legal codes of New Zealand. But back in March something happened there that keeps on running through my mind. Their House of Representatives, which must be a whole bunch different than ours, passed a bill giving human rights to the Whanganui River. How's that for treatment of a natural resource? Pretty good. And what I keep thinking—now that a river can claim personhood and dignity—is, What do I want to suggest for human rights next?

≈

Probably stars. They deserve to be noticed. Once a month we'll have darkness by decree. We'll have twelve new ways to look up, a dozen needed oases. And Puget Sound, of course. Whether seen from a ferry or not. Whether or not it's sundown on Seattle's million windows so the skyline is mirroring gold-orange, rose, and red, and the Olympic Mountains are both in front of you and behind you, and seagulls ride rivers of updraft, and this time and place and wind should be vested with rights. The trees near Crescent City too—they're older than Christianity. I'll call each redwood a cathedral, drinking fog, which truly is Holy Water. The snowmelt I drank in an ice cave: rights. Those ghost-conversations of coyotes: rights. That soul-blown sound of a train at night—part love, part loss, and part Coltrane—couldn't be more human, with the human right to quiet, so that everyone who needs to hear can hear.

≈

And what about you? Isn't there a lakeshore somewhere? Or a night in some December? Or a time you saw some pronghorn and were doubly surprised—first by their nearness, then a second time by how they leapt away: too squat to be bounding like that? Isn't there a long-distance drive you've taken with a good enough reason at the end of it? Or a kiss that lives in your memory, that goes on rivering and rivering? Or a view from the porch of a lightning storm coursing the sky?

≈

Anyway, it's April, soon to be summer in Utah, where most aren't yelling and opposed to helping refugees. Most don't think it's okay to zero them out, leave them trapped in their national horrors. In New Zealand they've granted more rights than that to a river, which ought to be an elemental lesson. Here's hoping it flows all the way from there to D.C.

IV.
9 TESTS

"WHAT'S MY FORTUNE?"

On the coast, you might spot
a minor griffin,

but your fury
will mistake it for a seagull.

Your anger makes beach fires
forbidden.

There are orcas,
but they'll go unseen.

Driftwood knows it's a floating letter—
I was there, now here,

then somewhere next—
but your hurt won't read it.

And the rest is hazy, uncertain,
so I'll just say this:

I have to eat fish skins too,
'til I'm full.

But not the bones.
They're too much work.

"FOR YOUR ESSAY,
DEFINE GREATNESS"

"If you grandstand,
you might still lose, funny man,"

was never a saying, but Paul's grandfather
said it all the time.

Like a holy scripture.
Like the measure of our size against the sun.

Another was "Time keeps running,
so better hug folks while you can.

Start with your grandfather,
leg it," by which he meant *now*.

Forty years as a mason.
This town

will stand for 200 more.
I'm not smart enough to rocket off

to Jupiter, but I'm not dumb;
I know how to listen.

It's a lot like watching with your ears,
while getting things done.

"FOR YOUR ESSAY, DEFINE INTELLIGENCE"

Kari's grandmother knew
the right words to explain.

She said, "Their ears can't listen.
They've traded their hearing

for a bigger make-believe mirror."
Deaf now, fixed

in four corners—that was her point.
Her heart first, mind second,

but almost a tie.
An absolute wisdom.

One time she took my hand
and said, "The day knows

many ways to tell you—
that blue jay,

a drop in the temperature—
and none are with a gun."

"FOR YOUR ESSAY,
DEFINE FREEDOM"

Millie's laugh could make you laugh,
her first gift among many.

Not everyone agreed.
"Get your horizon in line," they said,

but Millie
just rounded off a sunset.

"So, fräulein, you think you're a legend?"
She made a skiff out of playground sand.

Her mother used to worry,
used to dream about trapezes,

but one day, holding a pine cone
Millie sent her from around the world,

her mother smiled
and planted it. It grew fast.

And tall.
It catches snow.

"FOR YOUR ESSAY, DESCRIBE NATURE"

The screen door batters in its frame.
This is no June storm,

it's more
than a little wind,

so stand with your back against
whatever swear words you can.

Let them bloom.
Plant a garden.

If you had peaches, they'd be
flinging, nothing left:

wind-pilfered, engined
under.

You can lovetalk forever about nature.
It'll still kick your ass.

"FOR YOUR ESSAY, CHOOSE HALF FULL OR HALF EMPTY"

Even an empty shell is full
when you hold it to your ear,

the hollow inside like the kind
a cellist knows well—

full of song
that her bow hand remembers.

Song half wind, half steelhead
returning, song

from somewhere before.
Kelp washes up on the shore too. Drag it.

A fragment of mirror.
A lost key. A boat with one oar.

"WHAT GRADE WOULD YOU GIVE THE NIGHT?"

The stars are dialed in,
it's not noisy,

it smells full of life, late dinners
just over.

And a house set down in the middle
with a garden out back.

Someone calls to someone,
and the wind, that magic carpet, floats

her voice until it's everywhere,
and no dogs; *forget dogs*;

their barking seems packed off
to a museum

where people skip the headsets
since no one wants to hear.

I'd say it's a big Amen.
I'd love to trade places with an owl.

"OPEN 24 HOURS"

Our moon wasn't born
to look down at neon skies.

That was never in its forecast.
It can glow. And it predicts the tides,

those blue-green birthdays
always arriving.

It can pass for one minnow in the universe,
and yet still tell the sun, "Hold on,

just keep sitting in the east,
you aren't the driving song of astronauts.

I'm a medium,
the strange lines in their palms,

but to look at you
is to blink."

No wonder the moon
used to fire our legends.

What made us think
we can confiscate the night?

"WELL, WHAT CAN YOU DO ABOUT IT?"

You shouldn't look to challenge Cerberus,
but it's worse

to be a scarecrow.
Fight two of those hellhounds

with nothing but a pin—six heads
are better than none.

Call this a skin-and-bones protest,
say, "It's a song,

and you can't best
whatever king is reigning,"

but not today. The people are gathered.
Sometimes they win.

V.
9 ANSWERS

"WHAT'S IT LIKE LIVING BY THE OCEAN?"

At least one pier, and wind forever,
and weather that doesn't ask, "How are you?"

Grass in the sand dunes,
and sadness.

It never blows away.
It just keeps shifting around.

Everything is old here—cormorants,
the cliff face—

and everything old
is better than everything new,

like that plug-in lighthouse
with no one inside.

We don't mind questions, I guess.
But look out west and tell me that you don't know.

"TELL US A GHOST STORY"

When Paul's sister got laryngitis,
she started talking

through her crystal ball,
her hands as fast as a gunslinger.

Laugh,
but it worked. She even

saved someone,
signing *Fire* before we heard the sirens

and knowing where the ladder should go
to find the boy:

Tell them to hurry.
He's losing his pulse.

"But that's not a ghost story,
not if the boy didn't die."

The ghost is she never got her voice back.
She used to sing.

"TELL US A PARABLE"

One priest had a talent
for cataloging sin. A brain

like a laser.
No one minded

when he fell from a ladder
or wished they could feel more bad.

Another packed Mass like a stadium
but skipped six days of work.

He didn't make lunch for the daycare.
Forgot the old.

The smart priest
kept a garden:

seven boxes on his window sills,
larkspur

every shape and shade of fire—
better than homilies.

We loved to see them in the morning
as we drove by.

"WHAT'S THAT, SOME KINDA ALTAR?"

If you ask him for a reason—
"Why an altar to the rain?"—

you'll have to ask in a foreign language.
Not Dutch.

Not Spanish
or Bulgarian. I mean

on a drum. I mean
with your lifeblood thumping:

porch rail and sticks,
an upturned bucket,

just your hands.
His one rule is rhythm.

"And what will he say?"
He won't say anything,

but he'll join you on snare
or a bodhrán,

the two of you in his front yard,
sounding like rain.

"EVER WISH YOU WERE FAMOUS?"

I knew a man who made money
as a silhouette.

That outline standing upstream,
brilliantly backlit

by morning,
that was him.

The famous photo. Chin
to the north.

They've got a museum now somewhere,
and people signing the visitor's book.

About him, though,
I only hear rumors.

Something concerning the moon,
the next eclipse.

"TELL US A SECRET"

When night's aloft and the sky's
torn up,

someone's brother
has to journey.

Half *to*, half *from*, half
until doesn't matter

as long as the myths aren't skipped:
the gold cup, the hovering

firebird, the path
to the lake.

This is lightning,
and it wants a story.

This is summer, and it wants
more wine.

One time, I was the brother they sent;
that part isn't secret.

The storm took the shape of a woman.
That's the part that is.

"YOU DROPPED YOUR HOROSCOPE"

One morning the sun fell in love,
then changed its mind.

Life likes to go like that:
Now you're a planet, and next,

you're not a moon,
not an asteroid or radio wave, long gone

when the newspapers show up announcing,
"The Weather Today Calls for None."

Who can figure the sun's mind?
There was a poet once named Li Po.

Maybe he wrote it down somewhere:
the right words to fix the sky.

"TELL US ONE OF YOUR PROVERBS"

Even if you're an ocean
and you direct events—send rain

to a grassland,
stack lift-off winds

for the gulls to follow,
decide which hemisphere gets *Shipwreck*

and which gets *Violins
all night at a seaside recital*—still

you're a student forever,
dot dot dot.

That's what it means
to have the moon up there.

And even that moon
is studying the sun.

"TELL US ONE OF YOUR RITUALS"

In spring, we honor fire while everything
is green. We wait

for the eight signs—those upslope
boulders—to re-emerge from snow,

then stoke the bonfire
with all that needs to burn:

the husks of *One day*,
skeletons of *Yes*,

our dials
that only go from Medium

to Minus...
we turn them into heat and light and ash.

"Yeah?
And then what happens?"

Then the year starts over.
I never said we were different than the grass.

VI.

NORTH AND WEST OF WINNEMUCCA

Say you're adrift like I am.
Say it's 81 miles from this spot to Next Services,

plus or minus the sun in your eyes,
and a cloud—no, that's a contrail,

a plane out front like a dot. Like the pilot decided
to underline nothing at all,

just blue,
just whatever.

•

I'm not the unpaid extra in a saga, not the chef
at a long-forgotten inn,

though rain here is rare as a dragon
and *someone* paved this road;

they must have thought someone
was coming.

Call this Highway 140. Call it
Nevada. Call it

Earth. But I haven't seen a tree or a car
for an hour. Even the road signs

are alien: not Railroad Xing,
not a cow or a deer,

but burros and pronghorn antelope.
There's even one sign—no kidding—

left totally blank.
Just an empty yellow diamond.

Maybe it's supposed to mean Boredom Crossing.
Or maybe it's meant to match the radio: no news,

no preacher,
no mariachi signal.

Only me.
Whatever I add up to.

•

Somebody cut those stencils once,
and now they're never used

since who else, from here
to God's ladder, would ever have the need

for wild burros,
a herd of antelope?

They're probably stacked away
somewhere dusty. Or leaning

against a wall. And the future won't find them
and think they're hieroglyphics 'cause they're not.

•

Then suddenly it's Oregon. And nine miles in
it's a cliff. And now I can see

where those pronghorn are doing what they do:
52 hooves...maybe more...a dust cloud

sweeping up below.
So I figure this road started out as an antelope path,

then we came along and widened it.
One day we might add a guardrail too,

a metal stitch between *cars*
and *plunge*,

though those pronghorn wouldn't mind our wreckage;
they'd use it to scratch.

Rub up against.
A rest stop.

•

At last I come to the western edge:
Crescent City, California: redwoods

connecting the ocean to the sky.
It's dark, but I know they're there.

I know the water out front of me is cold,
so cold you'd have to be an otter

to go in.
And I can see four of them,

these *chitter-squeak* silhouettes, river otters
not the fat ones. They're visitors too.

Everything
must need the ocean.

•

There are birds here—stilts,
or killdeer, or something—spearing hermit crabs

out of the surf. The sound they make
isn't sparrow-song; it's better than that.

Behind me, trucks groan their air brakes...
this is Highway 101...

and southbound cars rev up
and find fifth gear.

Plus, every twelve seconds: the foghorn.
Every seventeen seconds: the waves.

And I know this isn't music,
but it's more than noise.

•

What will I do in the morning? Listen.
And what will I listen to? Waves.

I suppose you could call this
a sacrament; why not?

My dad died in April.
I keep on wishing we could talk.

He'd know why I noticed those otters
out of place,

downriver
with the snowmelt.

He'd tell me those birds are curlews, and he'd be right.
What I mean is I miss him.

•

There's probably someone you're missing too.
All I can say is I'm sorry.

There's a sign in Nevada that's blank.
Because they're gone.

VII.
9 CONCLUSIONS

"ANYTHING IN THE NEWS?"

Someone invents the diagonal
guitar—better

for leaning in the corner.
Another thinks night

is jumping the border of day.
He calls everything the morning.

A third man just has a daughter.
She's seven.

All he's doing
is teaching her to ride a bike.

"DO YOU BELIEVE IN ESP?"

If Paul's grandfather said, "Pack a jacket,"
there would be snow.

Even in April.
Even in May.

Call it *Farsight*, or *Weathergut*,
or just absentee voting from the North—

clouds would arrive like envelopes
and un-seal, un-tape,

un-whatever.
But we would be warm.

"MEETING TONIGHT: SUNDRESS OPTIONAL"

Summer is drafting an ordinance.
She writes, "Cold

can go sit in the corner."
She writes, "Cold can get busy

with waiting
'til it's time...

maybe think about salmon
or some other cold things in Alaska

like those birds they have
that aren't penguins. Anyway,

we're done. From now on winter
only comes to us in snow-cone form."

Like I said, it's just a draft.
She's got until seven to revise it,

which she can—find the right breeze to sway us,
each leaf like a plan.

"HE'S SUCH A GOOD LISTENER"

I knew a man who made money
from having three ears.

While some stood in line
at the plow shop, waiting for their turn

to get sharpened,
and golfers

hunkered on greens
and bells rang at school,

he performed the trick of listening
all afternoon.

Professional nods.
Some autopilot smiling...

His secret was that his third ear
cancelled out the others,

while also picking up the talk
of distant whales.

"FOR YOUR ESSAY, CONTRAST WANT AND NEED"

From Jonah to the Vikings,
from shipwrights

to kids in Middle Dakota
floating their splinters of balsa wood

downstream,
we need the ocean—

its wind
we can lean on,

its galaxies
close enough to reach,

and its just-right jaws for perspective:
unhinging,

and honest,
and somewhere under us with teeth.

"FOR YOUR ESSAY, COMPARE THE SKY TO A RIVER"

Hello, migration—bird after bird
pushing the wind around.

Down here
the moss is still green,

but I follow your point,
and I like your honking.

There's never less work to do, is there?
It's getting cold.

"RSVP ASAP"

If the future invites you
to dinner at eight,

leave now. It's hours
ahead of you,

having a drink on the veranda
and looking at the time.

The wine, the salmon—
better ask for them to go; already,

they've had years to get here.
All that long green

reaching. Those red scales
lunging up the falls.

"TELL US A BEDTIME STORY"

A *whirr* first
under the porch light

before you can see: a night-lost
hummingbird? a chunk

of fallen-down moon?
It can't be a moth, not *that* big,

but it is.
There's plenty to amaze you.

•

My cat likes lining them up
across the floor,

eight broken
accordions.

Then he looks at me
like *Make them play again.*

•

Here's a way to disorient:
Fly straight at the eye

and hover; that's a hummingbird.
And here's a way

to *seem* like you're running: downriver,
then wait like a pool.

•

Millie used to do that: run just ahead
and then turn.

She'd like these moths,
both fragile and fantastic,

like something from the pages of a book—
maybe one from her dinosaur shelf—

though I'm guessing is all.
We haven't talked in years.

•

What else will my cat attack?
Mice, of course, and birds,

and even a dog in the alley once:
ambush-leaping

from the fencepost.
Who knows why?

•

Rivers return forever—into clouds,
then into snowpack—

but the hummingbird moths
aren't coming back around.

Just a one-time
visitation.

•

I can tell from my cat: because
he's uncoiled now,

no longer crouched
for hunting.

And the whirring
is only traffic,

so that's that;
I can leave off the porch light.

The moon can cross from the grass
to the sidewalk.

The sirens
can take their slice of night.

Maybe some rain soon. Maybe tomorrow.
My cat will sleep.

"INSTEAD OF A HEADSTONE"

Kari's grandmother had her own way
to say *love*: "From Heaven

to the end,
from the Seven Lengths

until tomorrow."
So we said it

while letting her ashes
find the wind.

VIII.

CALL AND RESPONSE

"Give praise with the spider who builds a city out of her toes."[1]

We hear you, Reverend Sexton, and we say Amen.

"Praise with an ice cube for it will hold up miniature polar bears for a second."[2]

Again we hear you, Mother Anne, and we say Amen.

"I speak the password primeval, I give the sign of democracy, / By God! I will accept nothing which all cannot have their counterpart of on the same terms."[3]

And you're right, Father Whitman. Let your words be our national borders.

"I do not say these things for a dollar or to fill up the time while I wait for a boat."[4]

Nor do we.

---

1. From Anne Sexton's O Ye Tongues, specifically the "Seventh Psalm."

2. And again, this time from the "Ninth Psalm."

3. I'd say Walt Whitman's Song of Myself is like Ecclesiastes and then some, like the Bill of Rights and then some, like hitting the heart-brain jackpot every time you read. This is from the 24th section.

4. And this is from the 47th.

"Just once the kid with bad eyes hit a home run in an obscure sandlot game. You may ridicule the affectionate way he takes that day through a life drab enough to need it, but please stay the hell away from me."[5]

Hell yes, Richard Hugo. Keep preaching to the back rows of empathy. From Seattle to Missoula to everywhere east of the Rockies, we say Hell yes.

---

5. During the years that Richard Hugo worked for Boeing, the seats were bigger and the planes flew on time, and for the next two decades, when you looked out the window, you'd see angels, but they looked like herons, or like the women in the factory near my hometown in Washington. Women on the graveyard shift. Refugee women from Viet Nam, placing jars of pickles into boxes for America. For the burgers of backyard Texas. For the sandwiches on lunch trays in Kentucky. Which isn't part of Hugo's essay "In Defense of Creative-Writing Programs," but if you read behind the lines of *The Triggering Town*, it's there: write well, and remember what matters.

"I, too, sing America."[6]
And we listen, Minister Langston.
"I, too, am America."[7]
As are we, and we say Amen.

---

6. It's hard to believe Langston Hughes's poem "I, Too" isn't recited instead of the flag salute.

7. But why did that ever need asserting? And why does it still?

Thank you to the editors of the following journals in which these poems first appeared:

A3 Review 8 (April 2018): "Tell Us a Parable," winner of the November 2017 Poetry Contest.

Blue Earth Review 20 (2018): "He's Such a Good Listener."

Bluestem (May 2018): "What's My Fortune?"

Cobalt 20 (2018): "For Your Essay, Describe Nature"; "What Grade Would You Give the Night?"

Columbia Journal (8 July 2017): "Anything in the News?"; "Do You Believe in ESP?"; "Ever Wish You Were Famous?"

Crosswinds Poetry Journal 3 (2018): "Meeting Tonight: Sundress Optional."

Escape into Life (11 July 2018): "Well, What Can You Do about It?"

Escape into Life (11 Oct. 2017): "Tell Us a Bedtime Story."

Flock 19: Migration (2017): "For Your Essay, Define Freedom."

The Gateway Review: A Journal of Magic Realism 4.2 (2018): "Tell Us a Ghost Story."

Nightjar Review 5 (2018): "Tell Us One of Your Proverbs."

Pedestal Magazine 81 (2017): "Tell Us a Secret."

Poetry Northwest 13.2 (2019): "For Your Essay, Choose Half Full or Half Empty."

The Poet's Billow Literary Gallery (18 Aug. 2017): "Happy New Year!"; "How Do You Play? What's the Score?"; finalists for the 2017 Pangaea Prize (under the group title "Nothing to See Here, I'm Just Snowing").

Poets Reading the News (31 May 2018): "Call and Response."

Rock & Sling 12.2 (2017): "For Your Essay, Define Greatness."

saltfront 6 (2018): "For Your Essay, Define Intelligence"; "Open 24 Hours"; "Tell Us One of Your Rituals"; "What's It Like Living by the Ocean?"

Sheila-Na-Gig 2.3 (2018): "You Dropped Your Horoscope."

Sky Island Journal 1 (2017): "RSVP ASAP."

Sky Island Journal 2 (2017): "What's That, Some Kinda Altar?"

Snapdragon: A Journal of Art & Healing 3.4 (2017): "Instead of a Headstone."

Sugar House Review 11 (2019): "North and West of Winnemucca."

Sugar House Review 16 (2017): "I've Still Got My Passport"; "Still Works Good. Best Offer."

Terrain.org (9 Dec. 2018): "Tell Us One of Your Recipes" (as the poem ending "Extra Credit if You Read This at Work").

Terrain.org (29 Dec. 2017): "Are You Hungry"; "What Are Your Skills?" (as the opening and closing poems in "Poetry as Collage").

Terrain.org (27 May 2017): "Art Is Such a Good Journey" (as the poem ending "Wine Is Rain in Translation").

Terrain.org (26 Apr. 2017): "In the Beginning Was a River."

Terrain.org (23 Nov. 2016): "Poetic Justice."

Tilde 1.1 (2018): "For Your Essay, Contrast Want and Need."

Willow Springs 82 (2018): "When's My Luck Gonna Change?"

"In the Beginning Was a River" and "Tell Us an Origin Story" appeared as sections 1 and 2 of "Seven Rivers" in *Tales from the River*, Donna Mulvenna and Margi Prideaux, editors (Parndana, South Australia: Stormbird Press, 2018).

"In the Beginning Was a River" was reprinted in *The Dark Mountain Project*, Nick Hunt, editor (29 Aug. 2018), and in *About Place*

Journal: Dignity as an Endangered Species in the 21st Century, Pam Uschuk, editor (1 May 2019).

"For Your Essay, Compare the Sky to a River" appeared in *Routine: A Crack the Spine Themed Anthology*, Kerri Farrell Foley, editor (Galveston, TX: Crack the Spine, 2018).

"Tell Us a Parable" was nominated by the editors of *The A3 Review* for the Forward Arts Foundation's Forward Prize (for Best Single Poem published in the Republic of Ireland or the UK), 20 Feb. 2019.

Best of the Net 2018 nomination from *The Poet's Billow* for "How Do You Play? What's the Score?"

"Ever Wish You Were Famous," "Tell Us a Ghost Story," "Tell Us a Parable," "Tell Us a Secret," and "Tell Us One of Your Proverbs" were selected by Provo Poetry for inclusion in their POEMBALL machines in Provo, UT, in 2018-19. (Insert a quarter and out rolls a poem).

Rob Carney is the author of seven previous books of poems, including *Facts and Figures* (Hoot 'n' Waddle 2020), *The Last Tiger Is Somewhere* (Unsolicited Press 2020), co-authored with Scott Poole, and *The Book of Sharks* (Black Lawrence Press 2018), which won the 15 Bytes Utah Book Award for Poetry and was a finalist for the Washington State Book Award. *Accidental Gardens*, a collection of 42 flash essays about the environment, politics, and poetics, is forthcoming from Stormbird Press (Parndana, South Australia). Carney is the recipient of several honors for his work, including the Robinson Jeffers/Tor House Foundation Award for Poetry. He is a Professor of English at Utah Valley University and lives in Salt Lake City.